POLISH WINGS

Wojtek Matusiak

Supermarine Spitfire V
vol. 2

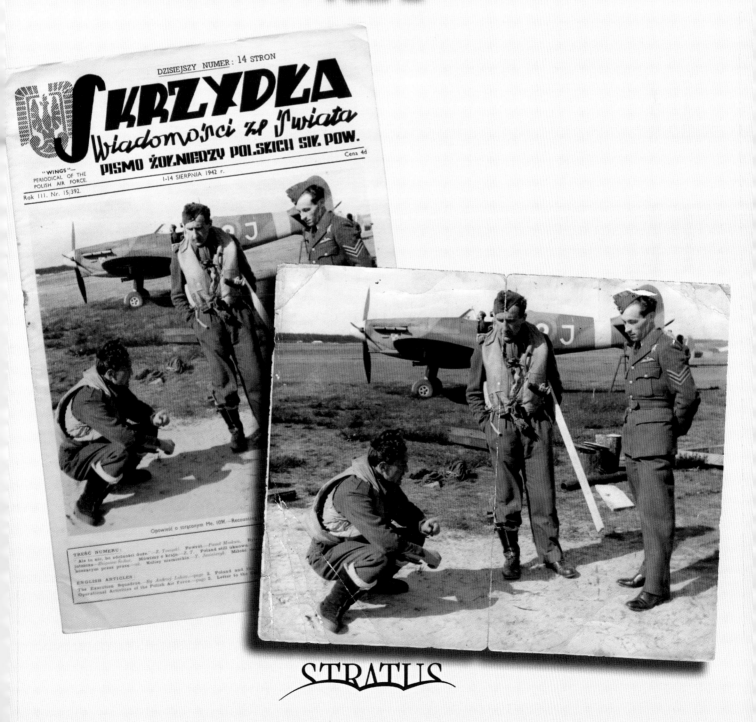

STRATUS

Wydawnictwo STRATUS s.j.
ul. Żeromskiego 4, 27-600 Sandomierz 1, Poland
e-mail: office@stratusbooks.pl
www.stratusbooks.com.pl
www.mmpbooks.biz

Copyright © 2021 Stratus,
Copyright © 2021 Wojtek Matusiak

ISBN 978-83-66549-30-2

Layout concept	Bartłomiej Belcarz
Cover concept	Artur Juszczak
Cover	Marek Ryś
Proofreading	Roger Wallsgrove
DTP	Wojtek Matusiak
	Stratus sp.j.
Colour Drawings	Robert Grudzień

PRINTED IN POLAND

Photograph credits:
Peter R. Arnold, Mark Baczkiewicz, Jim Brzózkiewicz, Zbigniew Charytoniuk, Tomasz Drecki, Zdeněk Hurt, Adam Jackowski, Michał Jaroszyński-Wolfram, Tomasz Kopański, Kornicki family, Wojciech Krajewski, Malcolm Laird, Wojciech Łuczak, Wojtek Matusiak, Miszkowicz family via M. Jagieniak, Peter Petrick, Jiří Rajlich, Wilhelm Ratuszyński, Mark Roguski, Piotr Sikora, Grzegorz Sojda, Nick Stroud, Szymankiewicz family, Andy Thomas, Olivier Tyrbas de Chamberet, Krzysztof Wagner, Wojciech Woźniakowski, Waldemar Wójcik, Wyszkowski family, Józef Zieliński, Wojciech Zmyślony, Imperial War Museum - London, Muzeum Lotnictwa Polskiego – Cracow, Muzeum Wojska Polskiego – Warsaw, Polish Institute and Sikorski Museum – London, Royal Air Force Museum – Hendon, Szkoła Podstawowa nr 11 – Ostrów Wielkopolski, ww2images.com.

My special thanks to Peter Arnold, Bob Sikkel and Wojciech Zmyślony (www.polishairforce.pl) for their invaluable assistance, and to Robert Grudzień, whose input was much more than just the colour plates.

Wojtek Matusiak

Previous page: Spitfire VB W3618 PK-J photographed at RAF Woodvale in the spring of 1942 with members of No. 315 Squadron, left to right: Sgt Marek Słoński, F/Lt Jan Falkowski and Sgt Mieczysław Matus. The photograph was then used on the cover of 'Skrzydła' ('Wings'), the Polish Air Force magazine, issue of 1–14 August 1942, captioned 'Recounting his victory over an Me. 109f' (even though, in fact, Sgt Słoński has never been credited with any aerial victories).

Front cover: A No. 317 Squadron Spitfire VB during Operation 'Starkey', a major allied exercise held in September 1943 to practice the invasion of France. During the exercise, aircraft of the 'invasion forces' received special markings in form of black and white bands on outer wing surfaces.

Back cover: Spitfire VB AB198 JH-T in the special scheme used during Operation 'Starkey'.

FPHU Model Maker
ul. Lotnicza 13/2, 78-100 Kołobrzeg, Poland
phone. +48 507-024-077 www.modelmaker.com.pl

Volume 1

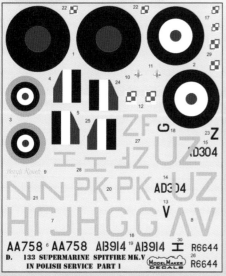

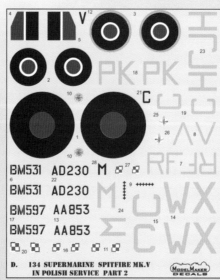

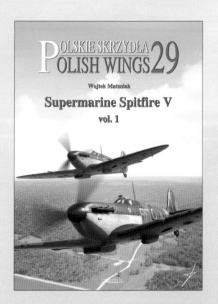

SUPERMARINE SPITFIRE V

No. 315 Squadron 'Dęblin'

In line with Nos. 306 and 308 Sqns of the 1st Polish Wing, No. 315 Squadron received its first Mk Vs in the last days of August 1941. At the time it was commanded by S/Ldr Stanisław Pietraszkiewicz. Full conversion onto the new variant was completed in early September and No. 315 was the first Polish squadron to fly these on operations from Northolt, when mixed Mk II/Mk V formations were sent for 'Circus 93' on the 1st (abortive due to weather) and on the 3rd (when it did proceed). All-Mk V operations commenced in the second half of the month. S/Ldr Pietraszkiewicz was shot down on 21 September during 'Circus 101', becoming a PoW. S/Ldr Władysław Szcześniewski took command of the squadron, but he, in turn, was downed during 'Circus 110' on 8 November 1941, joining his predecessor in captivity. S/Ldr Stefan Janus was appointed the new commander.

On 1 April 1942 the unit moved to Woodvale for a period of rest with the 2nd Wing (replaced by No. 317 at Northolt). It took its Spitfire Vs with it, as the variant was no longer in short supply and was also used by the resting units. At the beginning of May 1942 S/Ldr Janus was promoted to lead the 1st Polish Wing at Northolt and S/Ldr Mieczysław Wiórkiewicz took command of No. 315.

The unit returned to the 1st Wing at Northolt in the first days of September 1942, exchanging bases with No. 317 Sqn once again. This time the squadrons exchanged their aircraft as well, only the personnel moving between bases, but the Spitfire Vs remaining where they were. At the beginning of October S/Ldr Wiórkiewicz was posted to the HQ Fighter Command and S/Ldr Tadeusz Sawicz was appointed to command No. 315. In November 1942 the squadron re-equipped with Spitfire IXs.

On 1 June 1943, No. 315 Squadron, now commanded by S/Ldr Jerzy Popławski, moved to Hutton Cranswick, to join the 2nd Wing. In the process it left the Spitfire IXs behind for No. 303 Sqn, whose well-worn Mk Vs it now took with it.

Although the Squadron expected a routine resting period, during the month of June 1943 it continued to fly offensive operations from its new base. On 20 June it flew to Matlaske and exchanged aircraft with No. 19 Squadron RAF, taking over their LR.VB/VCs. At the beginning of July a reverse exchange took place, No. 315 receiving back most of the Mk VBs.

On 5 July the squadron flew these to RAF Ballyhalbert in Northern Ireland, where the period of rest from operations really commenced. This came to an end in November 1943, when the squadron left its Mk Vs for No. 303 Sqn there and moved back to Heston on the 13th. Here, it replaced No. 308 Sqn and took over its Mk Vs. It thus joined No. 133 Airfield/Wing which also included No. 306 Sqn. Both squadrons then continued to operate the LF/LR.Vs from Heston.

In mid-December 1943 No. 315 Squadron went to Llanbedr Armament Practice Camp in Wales for air-to-air gunnery training, which continued until the end of the year. New Year's Day saw No. 315 Sqn back at Heston. The old Spitfire Vs were showing increasing signs of wear, and accidents caused by all sorts of mechanical failures were becoming more and more frequent.

On 15 February 1944 S/Ldr Eugeniusz Horbaczewski took over from S/Ldr Popławski as the squadron commander.

In late March the squadron went to Llanbedr Armament Practice Camp again, this time for air-to-ground and dive bombing practice. Upon completion of the course the Spitfires were loaned to No. 129 Squadron RAF, which had joined No. 133 Wing and was going to undertake similar training. On 1 April 1944 No. 315 Sqn left RAF Heston to move to Coolham ALG where the entire wing re-equipped with North American Mustang IIIs.

[1]: Mk VB AB934, newly delivered to No. 315 in late August 1941, is inspected by F/Lt Stanisław Luranc, the squadron Engineer Officer (in the foreground). It displays the initial standard of Castle Bromwich-built Mk Vs, with the early type Rotol propeller (with blunt spinner and narrow-root metal blades). Coded PK-E, AB934 would be lost with F/O Jan Grzech during the tragic 'Low Ramrod 12' on 23 November 1941, when five pilots were killed and one severely wounded.

[2]: Supermarine-built Mk VB W3328 was first used by No. 611 Sqn. New Zealander ace F/Lt J.C.F. Hayter scored a 109 destroyed in it on 10 July 1941, but had to crash land after that combat. Repaired, W3328 was delivered to No. 315 Sqn in late September, becoming PK-T. During 'Circus 101' on 21 October its starboard wing was damaged by a direct cannon hit (Sgt Edward Jaworski flew it on that occasion). Note the style and arrangement of codes, the size and location of the Polish marking on the nose, and the black spinner backplate.

[3]: Spitfire VB BM597 PK-C (still airworthy today, registered G-MKVB) was built by the CBAF and delivered to No. 315 Sqn at Woodvale in early May 1942. After four months of service it was then transferred to No. 317 Sqn when the units exchanged bases in early September 1942 (see p. 44). P/O Lech Kondracki, shown here, also transferred from No. 315 to No. 317 at the time.

[4]: No. 315 Squadron pilots in front of one of their Spitfire VBs at Northolt in late March 1942. Left to right: Sgt Mieczysław Matus, F/Lt Jan Falkowski, Sgt Jan Adamiak, P/O Czesław Tarkowski, Sgt Jan Lipiński, F/O Włodzimierz Miksa, P/O Konrad Stembrowicz, F/O Franciszek Kornicki, S/Ldr Mieczysław Wiórkiewicz (deputy wing leader at Northolt), S/Ldr Stefan Janus, F/O Bolesław Sawiak, P/O Eugeniusz Malczewski, P/O Antoni Polek, Sgt Michał Cwynar, P/O Henryk Stefankiewicz, F/O Józef Gil (behind him), P/O Brunon Semmerling, Sgt Aleksander Chudek, Sgt Tadeusz Nawrocki, P/O Edward Jaworski.

[5, 6]: Spitfire VB BM561 PK-A was delivered to No. 315 Sqn at about the same time as BM597. Rather then being used by squadron pilots, though, it became the assigned personal Spitfire of the famous New Zealander ace, Colin Gray, who at the time held the post of Squadron Leader, Tactics, at the HQ of No. 9 Group. He used BM561 until September, when he was posted back on operations, and the Spitfire was taken over by No. 317 Sqn.

[7]: CBAF-built AD269 PK-R undergoing maintenance at RAF Northolt (in the southwestern dispersal area along the Western Avenue/A40, with the hangars visible across the airfield). This was an ex-No. 317 Sqn Spitfire (see p. 42), as were virtually all aircraft taken over by No. 315 upon arrival at Northolt in September 1942. It was used by No. 315 until early November, when the unit re-equipped with Spitfire IXs. AD269 then went to yet another Polish unit, No. 303, with which it was written off in a fatal accident on 15 December (see p. 95).

[8, 9]: AA762 PK-W, built by the dispersed Supermarine plants, was another ex-No. 317 Sqn Spitfire (see p. 42). On 11 September P/O Tadeusz Żurakowski (shown in the photos; not to be confused with the world-famous test pilot, Janusz Żurakowski) participated in an army/air force exercise, performing simulated attacks on ground troops near Western Avenue in Northolt. His Spitfire hit a concrete pillar and the bottom of the fuselage was torn open from the oil tank to the tail wheel. With no vital controls damaged he managed to get back and make a normal landing, but the Spitfire was written off immediately.

11

[10]: Gen. Kazimierz Sosnkowski, the C-in-C Polish Armed Forces visited RAF Ballyhalbert on 14 August 1943, when No. 315 Squadron Day was celebrated. This section escorting the VIP included F/O Edward Jaworski (AR338 PK-P, see p. 21) in the lead, with F/Sgt Stanisław Będkowski (BL970 PK-R) on his starboard wing, the other pair being W/O Mieczysław Matus (BL933 PK-M) and F/Sgt Kazimierz Łojek (W3937 PK-N).

[11]: Close escort was provided by W/O Stanisław Piątkowski (BM537 PK-T) with F/Sgt Jerzy Malec (BL993 PK-X) on the starboard…

[12]: …and F/O Stanisław Marcisz (AR451 PK-U) with P/O Stanisław Caliński (BL810 PK-Z) on the port side.

[13]: The airfield panorama on the same day featured BL469 PK-F and W3937 PK-N.
Note the marked differences in what was nominally Ocean Grey/Dark Green camouflage pattern on all these Spitfires. Also the presence or absence of various markings is noteworthy. Not only the Polish marking on the cowling and No. 315 Sqn triangular badge under the windscreen is missing on most of these aircraft, but BL933 PK-M even lacks the Sky band around the rear fuselage!

12

13

[14]: Snow-dusted Spitfire LR.VC AA968 PK-K lying in a Dutch field after the belly landing of P/O Roman Wal on 13 December 1943. The Spitfire had been used by No. 308 Sqn until 11 November when its Mk Vs were transferred to No. 315. AA968 was initially coded PK-G, but in December the code was changed to PK-K. It only flew one operational sortie in this guise: P/O Wal's ill-fated 'Ramrod 363' on Monday the 13th. The pilot was taken PoW. According to his post-war report, the engine developed a fault and when struggling to make it back he was attacked and damaged by a German fighter, which left him with no option but to crash-land near Gouda. Note the twisted metal blades of the de Havilland propeller (compare the condition of the wooden Rotol blades in photos 75-78, 262, or 263).

[15]: By the spring of 1944 the Spitfire V was obsolete, even if converted to the LF.V standard. The latter often involved fitting the exhausts with six outlets on each side. Here F/O Maciej Kirste poses with PK-F. This was W3412, built in the spring of 1941, a truly ancient aeroplane by wartime standards. Note the different style of codes introduced in late 1943.

[16]: A Spitfire V parked in a distant corner of Coolham ALG during April 1944 while No. 315 Sqn armourers attach a bomb to one of the new Mustangs. PK-I was probably BL259 which remained with the squadron until late April 1944. On 25 April F/Sgt Bolesław Czerwiński. flew No. 315 Sqn's last Spitfire, Mk VC EE659 PK-U, to No. 1 Civilian Repair Unit (CRU) at Cowley, thus ending the unit's association with the Supermarine fighter.

[17]: F/O Franciszek Kornicki in the cockpit of AB931 PK-C before the personal emblem was applied. He flew the Spitfire's first operational sortie on 4 September.

[18, 19]: Ground crew pose with AB931 PK-C at Northolt in September 1941. F/Sgt Czesław Marona is at the wing-root in both photos. LAC Stanisław Bączkiewicz is standing near the code letters in [18].

[20]: S/Ldr Władysław Szczęśniewski, who took command of No. 315 Sqn in late September and flew AB931 during his first operation in this capacity: 'Circus 103' on the 27th. The C on lower cowling was applied in red. Note that the Polish AF marking was still not applied when this photo was taken. The blunt spinner and narrow-root blades of the propeller, and the tear-drop shaped fairing on the side of the cowling, were standard on early CBAF production Mk Vs.

[21]: Another photo of ground crew with AB931 PK-C, with the dwarf emblem now visible near the cockpit. F/Sgt Marona is standing below the propeller. Note the absence of the Coffmann starter casing or any protruding component in the position of the tear-drop fairing. The 'C 315' stencil on the wheel chock is also worth noting.

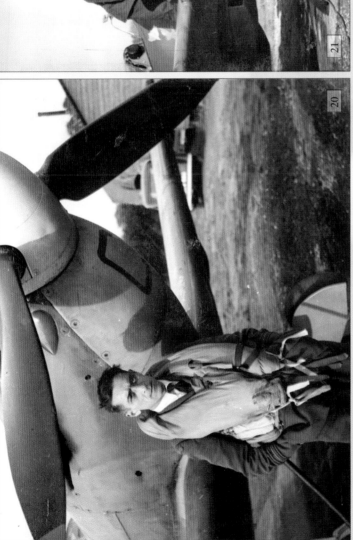

[22]: Spitfire VB AB931 PK-C, No. 315 Squadron, Northolt-Woodvale, September 1941-May 1942. Upper surface camouflage colours: Ocean Grey and Dark Green ('A' pattern); under surface colour: Medium Sea Grey.

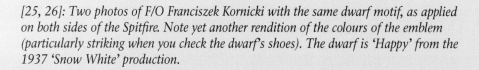

[23, 24]: *Contrary to a surprisingly widespread myth, there is no way to positively iden-tify various colours in a black-and-white photo. Two principal types of monochromatic negative material exist: panchromatic and orthochromatic. The former match human eye perception (reproducing yellow as a pale shade of grey, for example). Orthochromatic film enhances warm hues (so it rends yellow as an unnaturally dark grey shade, for example). Moreover, colour filters were commonly used in black-and-white photography in early/mid-20th century to enhance or suppress certain hues. These two consecutive frames were shot by the Polish Air Force Film Unit at No. 315 Sqn in early 1942. They depict Sgt Stanisław Laskowski, a visiting ferry pilot, in the cockpit of AB931. In photo [23] the pilot looks pale and the yellow ring of the roundel is as almost as light as the white one, while [24] seems to show a sun-tanned pilot and the yellow ring almost as dark as the red centre. The most striking item in this comparison is the dwarf personal emblem under the windscreen: its hues have changed completely. By comparing how each part of the artwork has changed here it is possible to make an educated guess at its real colours.*

[25, 26]: *Two photos of F/O Franciszek Kornicki with the same dwarf motif, as applied on both sides of the Spitfire. Note yet another rendition of the colours of the emblem (particularly striking when you check the dwarf's shoes). The dwarf is 'Happy' from the 1937 'Snow White' production.*

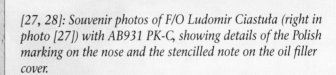

[27, 28]: Souvenir photos of F/O Ludomir Ciastuła (right in photo [27]) with AB931 PK-C, showing details of the Polish marking on the nose and the stencilled note on the oil filler cover.

[29, 30]: Wireless mechanics working on AB931 PK-C in late 1941 or early 1942 at Northolt. The Spitfire was usually flown by F/O Włodzimierz Miksa. On 21 October 1941 he was credited with a 109 destroyed, another probably destroyed and one more damaged, while flying it. A number of other pilots of No. 315 Sqn also flew AB931. On 8 December 1941 S/Ldr Stefan Janus used the Spitfire when he was credited with a Messerschmitt 109 destroyed. On 23 November 1941 P/O Konrad Stembrowicz escaped unscathed during the tragic 'Low Ramrod 12', although the elevator was shot up. The same pilot flew AB931 during the squadron move to Woodvale on 1 April 1942.

[31]: AB898 was another CBAF-built Mk VB delivered to No. 315 Sqn in the last days of August 1941. This photo was taken before the Polish marking was applied on the nose.

[32, 33]: In 1941 P/O Zygmunt Drybański was the regular pilot, but between late January and April 1942 the Spitfire was usually flown by F/O Kornicki, shown here with two ground crew members. LAC Mieczysław Kubalski is on the right in both photos, but the other fitter (seated on the wing in [32] and standing on the other side of the fuselage in [33]) has not been identified. By that time the Polish marking had been applied on the nose. Note also the aircraft letter on the bottom of the cowlings, presumably in red. The Spitfire was fitted with an interim Rotol propeller that combined the early-style blunt spinner with the late broad-root blades made of wooden composite material.

[34]: AB898 PK-I photographed at the same location after the Polish Air Force marking was applied on the nose. Note how the colours of the roundel look different due to another type of negative and/or colour filter used. Like all early Spitfire VBs it had left factory in the Temperate Land scheme (Dark Earth and Dark Green). When the colour scheme changed on day fighters in August, the Dark Earth areas were resprayed at No. 45 Maintenance Unit (MU) with a shade of grey that was obviously darker than the regulation Ocean Grey.

[35]: Spitfire VB AB898 PK-I, No. 315 Squadron, Northolt-Woodvale, September 1941 – May 1942. Upper surface camouflage colours: unspecified dark grey in place of Ocean Grey, and Dark Green ('A' pattern); under surface colour: Medium Sea Grey.

[36]: *Spitfire VB W3618 PK-J, No. 315 Squadron, Northolt-Woodvale, October 1941 – June 1942. Upper surface camouflage colours: Ocean Grey and Dark Green ('A' pattern); under surface colour: Medium Sea Grey.*

36

37

[37]: W3618 was one of the last Mk Vs built by the parent Supermarine factory to be fitted with the early style windscreen. RAF documents say it was originally delivered to No. 72 Sqn RAF in late August 1941, but transferred to No. 315 soon afterwards. This might be a clerical error, though, as W3516 was, indeed, used (and lost) by No. 72 at the time. When this photo was taken in late 1941 or early 1942, the Spitfire was definitely in use with the Polish unit at Northolt, coded PK-J. The ground crew members in the photo are, sadly, unrecognized while the three pilots, wearing their 'Mae-Wests', are, left to right: P/O Konrad Stembrowicz, F/O Włodzimierz Miksa and Sgt Jan Kowalski. The serial number is in the regulation size, as applied at No. 39 MU. The J with a prominent horizontal bar was typical in No. 315 codes at the time. Initially flown by various pilots, in mid-November it was 'acquired' by S/Ldr Stefan Janus, the new commander of the squadron. On his first operational sortie with No. 315, the ill-fated 'Low Ramrod 12' on 23 November, the Spitfire was damaged, but was repaired within days. Janus then used it until his departure from the unit in early May 1942. It was then taken over by his successor, S/Ldr Mieczysław Wiórkiewicz, until early June, when it was sent away for a scheduled overhaul. It was then converted to a 'hooked Mk VB' standard and spent the rest of its life with the FAA.

38

39

[38]: W3618 PK-J at RAF Woodvale with members of No. 315 Squadron, left to right: Sgt Marek Słoński, F/Lt Jan Falkowski and Sgt Mieczysław Mattus. The shot was obviously staged by official Polish AF photographers (see the title page of this book) and it is not clear what is the purpose of the long plank that F/Lt Falkowski is holding under his arm... Note that by the time of this photo the serial had been reapplied in small-size characters on the Sky band, but the camouflage pattern seems unchanged otherwise.

[39]: The same Spitfire refuelled at Woodvale. The style of the serial number is shown to advantage.

16

[40]: AD262 was a CBAF-built Mk VB first delivered to No. 315 in late September 1941. Coded PK-M it was soon damaged in an accident on 2 October, with G/Cpt Stefan Pawlikowski (the Senior Polish Liaison Officer to HQ Fighter Command RAF, i.e. the head of the entire Polish AF fighter force in Britain) at the controls. Following repairs at No.71 (Repair & Salvage) MU at Slough, it resumed service with the same squadron in November, now coded PK-U. Its subsequent service with the unit was uneventful, except for a minor incident on 13 February 1942, when Sgt Kazimierz Zielonka popped it up onto its nose at Northolt. This photo was taken at this Middlesex base in late 1941 or early 1942. Note how the Sky band was aligned with the rear frame of the fuselage. Clear signs of touching-up the finish can be seen on the fin and near the code letters. The IFF wire aerial between the tip of the tailplane and the fuselage is shown very clearly.

40

[41]: *Spitfire VB AD262 PK-U, No. 315 Squadron, Northolt-Woodvale, November 1941-June 1942. Upper surface camouflage colours: Ocean Grey and Dark Green ('A' pattern); under surface colour: Medium Sea Grey.*

[42]: *AD262 PK-U at Woodvale in the summer of 1942. This view shows that it featured the standard and late-style Rotol propeller with the broad-root blades and long pointed spinner. Note the oversize underwing roundels: when the style of the British markings was changed in June, the new 'C' style insignia were supposed to be much smaller than the old 'A' style one. But in this case the overall size was unchanged, and portions of the original broad white ring were overpainted blue and red. This was also seen on other Spitfires used by No. 315 Sqn at the time (see BM597 on p. 44). AD262 soldiered on with No. 315 Squadron until transferred to No. 317 in early September (see pp. 56-57).*

[43]: *Spitfire VB AR424 PK-C, No. 315 Squadron, Northolt, September–November 1942.*
Upper surface camouflage colours: Ocean Grey and Dark Green ('A' pattern);
under surface colour: Medium Sea Grey.

[44, 45]: AR424 was a typical Westland-built Spitfire VB, fitted with the de Havilland propeller, easily recognisable by its short pointed spinner and slim metal blades. Until early September 1942, this was the personal mount of No. 317 Sqn 'A' Flight Commander, F/Lt Marian Trzebiński, coded JH-A. When the units exchanged bases and aircraft, it was taken over at Northolt by the 'A' Flight Commander of No. 315, F/Lt Franciszek Kornicki. Now coded PK-C, AR424 was his mount until the squadron re-equipped with Spitfire IXs in November 1942. These souvenir photos were obviously taken by ground crew members during a visit of Polish Navy sailors. Note that, rather than just alter the codes, the Spitfire seems to have been given a complete repaint: the RAF roundel on the fuselage is positioned unusually far forward, and the colour pattern on the nose is not quite standard. The serial number was re-applied with a small-size stencil about mid-way up the Sky band. Note also '315 FL. A' painted on the wheel of the start-up trolley.

45

[46]: *Spitfire VB BL670 PK-B, No. 315 Squadron, Hutton Cranswick-Ballyhalbert, June–August 1943. Upper surface camouflage colours: Ocean Grey and Dark Green ('A' pattern); under surface colour: Medium Sea Grey.*

[46]

[47, 48]: *A solemn mass was celebrated during No. 315 Squadron Day festivities on 14 August 1943. An altar was erected in a hangar at RAF Ballyhalbert, flanked by two Spitfires. BL670 PK-B had previously served with No. 303 Sqn, first as RF-K 'Krysia' (see vol. 1, pp. 43–46) and then as RF-B. When the units exchanged aircraft on 1 June 1943, No. 315 simply replaced the squadron code and obliterated No. 303's badge near the windscreen. The Polish AF square on the nose was left in the position that was typical for the previous operators. Note the clipped wing tip, although the Spitfire was not an LF conversion. BL670 then continued to be used by No. 315 until November 1943, when it was handed back to No. 303 Sqn at Ballyhalbert. A month later it was transferred to the USAAF.*

[48]

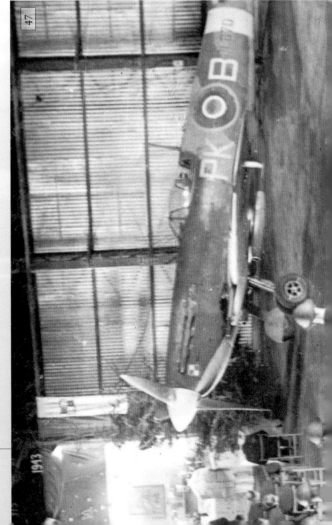

[47]

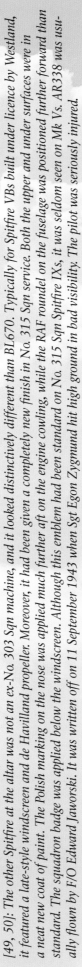

[49, 50]: The other Spitfire at the altar was not an ex-No. 303 Sqn machine, and it looked distinctively different than BL670. Typically for Spitfire VBs built under licence by Westland, it featured a late-style windscreen and de Havilland propeller. Moreover, it had been given a completely new finish in No. 315 Sqn service. Both the upper and under surfaces were in a neat new coat of paint. The Polish marking on the nose was applied much further aft on the engine cowling, while the RAF roundel on the fuselage was positioned further forward than standard. The squadron badge was applied below the windscreen. Although this emblem had been standard on No. 315 Sqn Spitfire IXs, it was seldom seen on Mk Vs. AR338 was usually flown by F/O Edward Jaworski. It was written off on 11 September 1943 when Sgt Egon Zygmund hit high ground in bad visibility. The pilot was seriously injured.

[51]: Spitfire VB AR338 PK-P, No. 315 Squadron, Ballyhalbert, July-September 1943. Upper surface camouflage colours: Ocean Grey and Dark Green ('A' pattern); under surface colour: Medium Sea Grey.

[52]: Spitfire VB EN788 PK-C, No. 315 Squadron, Ballyhalbert, July–October 1943. Upper surface camouflage colours: Ocean Grey and Dark Green (approx. 'A' pattern); under surface colour: Medium Sea Grey.

[53, 54]: Gen. Kazimierz Sosnkowski, the C-in-C Polish Armed Forces, and other guests of the unit were entertained with an elaborate display of formation flying during the Squadron Day celebrations on 14 August. This is F/Lt Czesław Tarkowski landing in Spitfire VB EN788 PK-C, his usual mount, after the performance. This aeroplane must have also been repainted completely, as the camouflage is only a very rough approximation of the regulation 'A' pattern. Note yet another arrangement of markings: although the roundel retained its standard position, the squadron code was applied near the tail and the aircraft letter at the cockpit. There is no Polish AF marking or squadron badge.

[55]: *AVM Mateusz Iżycki, AOC Polish AF, salutes the Polish Air Force colours during a ceremony at Heston on 6 February 1944.*

[56]: *G/Cpts Ludwik Szul-Skjöldkrona (Senior Polish Liaison Officer at the HQ 2nd Tactical Air Force) and Mieczysław Mümler (Senior Polish LO at the HQ No. 84 Group 2nd TAF) during the same ceremony. Spitfire VB EP646 PK-Z can be seen in the background of both photos. It was a Mk VB built by the CBAF in mid-1942. Following service with RAF units, it was delivered to No. 133 Wing at RAF Heston in December 1943, going to No. 315 Sqn where it was usually flown by F/O Michał Cwynar. During the wing's move from Heston to Coolham ALG on 1 April 1944 it was flown by F/Sgt Bolesław Czerwiński. The next day it logged the last operational sortie ever flown by a Spitfire of No. 315 Sqn, with F/O Jerzy Polak at the controls (notably, it was a scramble of two aircraft followed by a Channel patrol, but the other pilot, F/Sgt Tadeusz Słoń, was flying a borrowed No. 129 Sqn Spitfire LF.VB, EN922 DV-Q).*

[57]: *Spitfire VB EP646 PK-Z, No. 315 Squadron, Heston, January–April 1944. Upper surface camouflage colours: Ocean Grey and Dark Green ('A' pattern); under surface colour: Medium Sea Grey.*

23

No. 316 Squadron 'City of Warsaw'

Like other squadrons of the 2nd Polish Wing at the time, No. 316 started conversion from Hurricane IIs to Spitfire Vs in October 1941. At the time it was based at RAF Church Stanton and commanded by S/Ldr Wacław Wilczewski. He failed to return from 'Circus 110' on 8 November 1941, becoming a PoW. S/Ldr Aleksander Gabszewicz took over as the new commander.

On 12 December the squadron moved to Northolt, joining the 1st Wing. It left its Mk Vs behind at Church Stanton for No. 306 Sqn, and took over another set of virtually identical Mk Vs at Northolt that had been left there by No. 308. Following the winter lull, No. 316 Squadron flew intensive operations with the 1st Polish Wing throughout the spring and early summer 1942. On 23 April it moved to RAF Heston, which became a satellite of Northolt. In the first week of June 1942 Gabszewicz was replaced by S/Ldr Janusz Żurakowski (who later became a famous test pilot) at the head of No. 316 Sqn. Between 30 June and 7 July the unit was temporarily based at Croydon for the expected Operation 'Rutter', which failed to materialise.

In the last days of July 1942 No. 316 left Heston for a period of rest with the 2nd Wing, taking its Spitfire Vs to Hutton Cranswick. Between 15 and 20 August it replaced No. 303 at Kirton-in-Lindsey (while the latter squadron took part in Operation 'Jubilee'). No. 316 then returned to Hutton Cranswick. At the end of December 1942 S/Ldr Marian Trzebiński took over command of the squadron.

On 12 March 1943 No. 316 returned to Northolt, exchanging places and aircraft with No. 306 Squadron: the former re-equipped with ex-No. 306 Spitfire IXs, while the latter unit took over its Mk Vs in the 2nd Wing.

No. 316 Squadron, now commanded by S/Ldr Paweł Niemiec, reverted to Mk Vs once more in September 1943, when its tour of duty with the 1st Wing ended. On the 21st the squadron's Mk IX were left at Northolt for No. 302, while No. 316 re-equipped with ex-No. 306's LF.Vs and moved to RAF Acklington. It thus became part of the token 3rd Fighter Wing of the Polish Air Force. In mid-February 1944 No. 316 Sqn moved to Woodvale. It soldiered on with the obsolete Mk Vs until re-equipment with Mustang IIIs in April 1944.

[58]: *W3945 was a Supermarine-built Mk VB delivered brand new to No. 317 Sqn in the 2nd Polish Wing in October 1941. A month later it was transferred to No. 316 Sqn and coded SZ-H. Following a few weeks of uneventful service it was handed over, with all No. 316's Spitfires, to No. 306 when it replaced No. 316 at RAF Church Stanton on 12 December. It was lost on the 30th with F/Lt Stanisław Zieliński during Operation 'Veracity II' to Brest.*

[59]: *This seemingly anonymous Spitfire VB, believed to be BL303 SZ-E, displays No. 316 Sqn's standard arrangement of markings on the port side: code letters near the cockpit, squadron badge at the top of the fuselage immediately aft of the cockpit, and the Polish AF red-and-white square with 'POLAND' below applied on the engine cowling below the rear exhaust section. The ground crew posing with the aircraft are, sadly, unrecognized, except for Sgt Paweł Kulesza, standing second right.*

[60, 61]: *From 1941 until early 1943, the codes on No. 316 Sqn Spitfire Vs were applied in the same sequence on both sides: SZ followed by the aircraft letter, as shown here on AB971 SZ-C in early 1942. In the ground shot, 2ⁿᵈ Lt Bełtta of the Polish Army, attached as ground defence officer to the squadron, poses with the Spitfire. Note prominent traces of overpainted previous operator's codes (AB971 had earlier flown with No. 19 Sqn RAF). The white triangle seems empty in both shots, ready for the application of the badge.*

[62, 63]: *No. 316 was heir to traditions of the pre-war IV/1 Dywizjon Myśliwski (IV/1 Fighter Squadron) of the Warsaw-based 1ˢᵗ Air Regiment, so initially its flights used two different emblems on their Hurricanes and Spitfires. Aircraft of the 'A' Flight (marked with letters from the first half of the alphabet) featured the 'Owl' badge of the 113 Eskadra (113ᵗʰ Flight), as shown here on AB920 SZ-K, the personal Spitfire of the Flight Commander, F/Lt Tadeusz Sawicz (posing in the middle). 'B' Flight aircraft (identified with letters from the second half of the alphabet) used 114 Eskadra's 'Swallow' motif in their triangular badge, as shown on AD363 SZ-R (P/O Tadeusz Dobrut-Dobrucki, wearing 'Mae-West' here, was shot down and killed in the Spitfire on 28 February 1942).*

[64]: *The style of code letters was standardised during 1942, as shown on EN917 here, which succeeded AB920 as the new SZ-K. Following departure of F/Lt Sawicz this code was 'acquired' by F/O Jerzy Szymankiewicz, who had his personal nickname 'Maskota' applied near the cockpit. He is standing first right here, joking with the chief mechanic F/Sgt Bronisław Pianko, while P/O Bolesław Gęca is resting on the wing.*

[65]: *In February 1942 it was decided to adopt the 'Owl' as the sole emblem of No. 316 Sqn and subsequently this motif was applied on aircraft of both flights, as shown in this photo of F/O Józef Dec with 'B' Flight's Mk VB W3759 SZ-Z.*

[66]: When No. 316 Sqn re-equipped with ex-No. 306 Spitfire IXs in March 1943, the sequence of codes on the starboard side of the fuselage was reversed, and the squadron letters were now applied near the cockpit on this side, too. A few Mk VBs continued to be used as hacks, and this is one of these, probably AD425 SZ-O.

[67]: In September 1943 No. 316 gave up its Mk IXs, reverting to Spitfire Vs. At the same time the squadron badge started to be applied below the windscreen, as shown in this photo of 'B' Flight pilots in December 1943 at Digby. Posing, left to right: F/Sgt Tadeusz Szymański, F/Sgt Stefan Sztuka, F/O Lew Kuryłowicz, F/Lt Bolesław Kaczmarek, F/O Stanisław Litak, F/Sgt Czesław Bartłomiejczyk, Sgt Zygfryd Narloch, and F/O Eugeniusz Szaposznikow.

[68]: In April 1944 No. 316 Sqn re-equipped with North American Mustang IIIs, giving up its worn-out Spitfire Vs. This is BM587 SZ-D or BM588 SZ-Q upon transfer to No. 63 Sqn RAF at the beginning of May 1944, still in full markings of the Polish unit.

[69]: *Spitfire VB AA858 SZ-D, No. 316 Squadron, Church Stanton, October–December 1941. Upper surface camouflage colours: Ocean Grey and Dark Green ('A' pattern); under surface colour: Medium Sea Grey.*

69

70

[70]: *This Supermarine-built Mk VB was delivered brand new to No. 316 Sqn at Church Stanton. It displayed a standard set of 'A' Flight markings at the time, including the 'Owl' emblem of the pre-war 113 Eskadra (not yet adopted as the badge of the entire No. 316!) and the Polish square on the nose with 'POLAND' stencilled beneath. It was usually flown by F/O Józef Górski. In December 1941 the Spitfire was transferred to No. 306 Sqn when the latter replaced No. 316 in the 2nd Polish Wing. Its further story is described in vol. 1 on p. 70.*

[71]: *Although not looking very impressive in this photo, taken at Northolt following a taxiing accident of Sgt Władysław Kiedrzyński on 13 February 1942 (the damage was minimal), Supermarine-built W3798 was a successful machine in the hands of Polish pilots. Delivered brand new to No. 308 Sqn at Northolt in early September 1941, it was credited with three victories: a Messerschmitt 109 destroyed by S/Ldr Marian Pisarek on 13 October, a 109 probably destroyed by F/Lt Marian Wesołowski on 21 September, and a 109 damaged by F/O Jerzy Popławski on 8 November 1941. On 15 November the latter pilot suffered a serious landing accident in it but escaped injury. A month later W3798 was transferred to No. 316 Sqn, which replaced No. 308 at Northolt. It is likely that it was initially adorned with 114 Eskadra's 'Swallow' before the 'Owl' was adopted as No. 316 Sqn emblem. The Spitfire showed clear traces of overpainted ZF codes of No. 308, but the Y was unchanged (on this side at least) since No. 308 Sqn times. On 3 May 1942 the Spitfire was flown by P/O Czesław Jaworowski (its usual pilot at the time) when he was credited with an FW 190 destroyed. At the end of that month it left No. 316 for a major inspection and was subsequently used by a number of RAF squadrons. In September 1943 it was one the last Mk Vs on charge of No. 317 Sqn, but next month it was re-categorised as a Ground Instructional Airframe (4263M).*

[72]: *Spitfire VB W3798 SZ-Y, No. 316 Squadron, Northolt, December 1941–February 1942. Upper surface camouflage colours: Ocean Grey and Dark Green ('A' pattern); under surface colour: Medium Sea Grey.*

[73]: Spitfire VB AD130 SZ-E, No. 316 Squadron, Northolt, December 1941–April 1942. Upper surface camouflage colours: Ocean Grey and Dark Green ('A' pattern); under surface colour: Medium Sea Grey.

[74]: AD130 was built by CBAF and delivered to No. 308 Sqn when it re-equipped with the variant in early September 1941. Like all other Spitfires of the unit, it was left at Northolt in December for No. 316 Sqn during the squadron exchange. This photo of P/O Kazimierz Samofał was taken at Northolt in late 1941 or early 1942. Note the hard colour division lines, not seen on factory applied finish. The Spitfire had undergone repairs at Heston Aircraft Ltd in October 1941 and that was probably when the repainting took place.

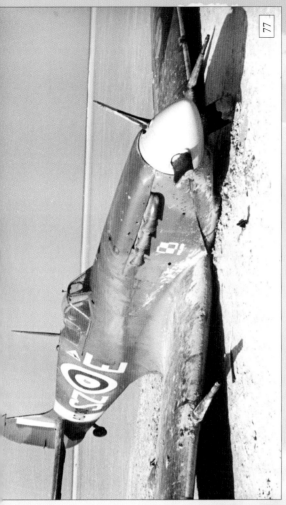

77

76

78

[75–78]: AD130 SZ-E was usually flown by F/Os Józef Dec and Bernard Buchwald. On 10 April 1942 Dec used it when he claimed an FW 190 probably destroyed, but two days later Buchwald went down in it in France when the squadron was engaged by Focke-Wulfs. His colleagues assumed he was shot down in combat, but in his post-war ex-PoW report he blamed an engine failure (notably all three wooden blades of the Rotol propeller were completely broken, indicating that the engine worked on impact). Note that the colour division lines are of the standard soft kind. Those on the rear fuselage are even softer than usual, probably due to obliterating previous codes, when the new squadron code replaced No. 308 Sqn's aircraft letter and vice versa.

[79]: P/O Mieczysław Wyszkowski on a seemingly anonymous Spitfire VB coded SZ-S in early 1942. Its identity can be ascertained from the circumstances of the shot, taken after he scored a victory in this aeroplane. Three confirmed 'kills' were credited to Wyszkowski, all during March/April 1942, and on each occasion he was flying Spitfire VB W3718 SZ-S. He flew it on 13 March when he was credited with a Messerschmitt 109 destroyed, on 10 April when he scored one Focke-Wulf 190 destroyed and another damaged, and during the morning mission on 25 April 1942 he was credited with another 190 confirmed destroyed. On the latter date in the afternoon F/Lt Stanisław Skalski used the same Spitfire when he was credited with a 109 damaged. Note the 'S', probably in black, on the bottom cowling under the spinner.

[80, 81]: Two more photos of the same Spitfire, probably taken on the same occasion, with F/O Włodzimierz Klawe on the open cockpit door. He also flew the Spitfire repeatedly in late March and early April 1942.

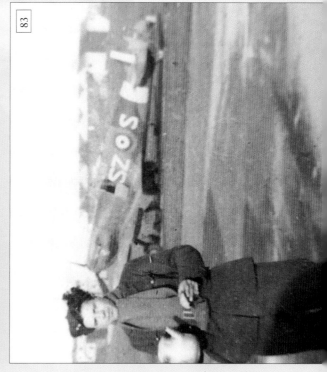

[82]: *Spitfire VB W3718 SZ-S, No. 316 Squadron, Northolt, January–April 1942. Upper surface camouflage colours: Ocean Grey and Dark Green ('A' pattern); under surface colour: Medium Sea Grey.*

[83, 84]: *Two more photos of the Spitfire taken at about the same time at Northolt. Note the hard colour division lines on the fuselage, where code had been changed several times. When W3718 was delivered to No. 316 in January 1942, the Spitfire had already served with two other Polish units. In September 1941 the Supermarine-built machine was allocated to No. 306 Sqn at Northolt, a month later going to No. 303. It seems that the serial number was obliterated on the fuselage during subsequent re-codings. Note that, even though the photos were taken after several months of service with No. 316 Sqn, the Spitfire did not have the unit's badge applied. In late April Sgt Tadeusz Szymański became another regular pilot of W3718 and it was he who took it to No. 1 CRU at Cowley on 20 May; thus ending the Spitfire's Polish service. The machine was subsequently used by a number of British and Allied units (including the 4th FS 52nd FG USAAF and No. 340 'Free French' Sqn RAF), until written-off in an accident in April 1945.*

[85]: *Spitfire VB BL646 SZ-R, No. 316 Squadron, Northolt, March–June 1942.*
Upper surface camouflage colours: Ocean Grey and Dark Green
('A' pattern); under surface colour: Medium Sea Grey.

[86, 87]: *No. 316 Sqn members: F/O Jerzy Radomski and Ryś take turns posing on BL646. This was one of several dozen Spitfires paid for by the Far Eastern Dutch community via the Prins Bernard Fond. Muntok is a town on the island of Bangka in the Dutch East Indies, now Indonesia (to a Polish eye it might look like a man's name, resembling such popular first names at the time as Mundek and Wojtek). The note inside the cockpit door: 'MAKE SURE DOOR IS / LOCKED BEFORE FLIGHT' was applied in a position that was standard for this batch of CBAF-built Spitfires.*

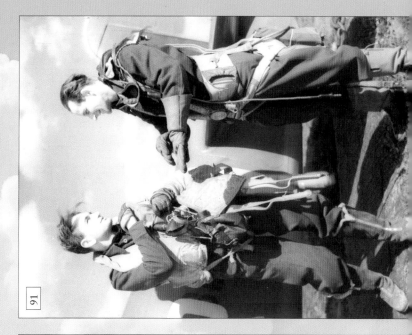

[88]: *No. 316 Sqn Spitfires taking off from Northolt in early 1942. Note the arrangement of the code letters on the starboard side of the fuselage. SZ-R is believed to be BL646, with the name 'MUNTOK' applied in the standard style and position on this side as well. F/Lt Stanisław Skalski, reposted to No. 316 Sqn in March 1942 to command the 'B' Flight, chose this brand new Mk VB as his personal mount. BL646 replaced AD363 lost in February (see p. 25) as the new SZ-R. Skalski scored a Focke-Wulf 190 destroyed on 10 April and another probably destroyed on 3 May in the Spitfire. On 5 May 1942 Sgt Władysław Kiedrzyński used BL646 to score an FW 190 destroyed and on 3 June P/O Wyszkowski was credited with an FW 190 probably destroyed. BL646 was used by No. 316 Sqn until late 1942 and then, following some repairs and modification to LF.VB, returned to the unit in late 1943.*

[89]: *A group of No. 316 Sqn pilots in joking mood photographed by the Spitfire BL646 SZ-R in the spring of 1942. Right to left: P/O Jerzy Szymankiewicz, P/O Zdzisław Przygodzki, Sgt Kazimierz Gawlewicz, P/O Mieczysław Wyszkowski and (upside down) P/O Antoni Chołajda. The aircraft letter beneath the propeller is shown to advantage.*

[90]: *P/O Władysław Balon photographed in April 1942 by a No. 316 Sqn Spitfire VB believed to be BL646 SZ-R. The squadron code and badge are well visible.*

[91]: *Another photo taken on the same occasion: P/O Balon (left) and F/O Włodzimierz Klawe by the side of BL646. The serial, partly covered by aircraft letter R, is just visible in Balon's shadow.*

[92]: *Spitfire VB AR434 SZ-J, No. 316 Squadron, Northolt–Hutton Cranswick, June 1942–January 1943. Upper surface camouflage colours: Ocean Grey and Dark Green ('A' pattern); under surface colour: Medium Sea Grey.*

[93]: Fitter AC1 Czesław Olszewski and Spitfire VB BL646 SZ-R (note the R on the bottom cowling and the presentation name 'MUNTOK'). Another Mk VB, AR434 SZ-J, can be seen in the background.

[94]: A similar scene with more men working on the engine of, presumably, AR434. The aircraft letter J can be made out on the bottom cowling panel, and it is also applied on the starter trolley. F/Sgt Bronisław Pianko is holding the tip of the propeller blade on the left, while Sgt Paweł Kulesza is standing near the port wing cannon, looking at something on the ground. These two photos offer good comparison of the Rotol (BL646) and de Havilland (AR434) propellers.

[95]: P/O Stanisław Litak with AR434 SZ-J. The Spitfre, licence-built by Westland, was delivered brand new to No. 316 Sqn in mid-June 1942. Litak was one of its regular pilots. The significance of the emblem on the rudder is not known. The S-coded Spitfre in the background, to the left of Litak, is AB278, which succeeded W3718. The Spitfire visible to the right of Litak (serial or code not known) seems to have an individual emblem below the windscreen.

[96]: An unrecognised ground crew member posing with the Spitfire on the same occasion. The squadron code and badge were applied in the usual fashion of the period. The cockpit hood framing seems partly unpainted. AR434 went to No. 1 CRU for a major overhaul in late January 1943. After a period of storage it was delivered to No. 315 Sqn in mid-June, only to be seriously damaged in an accident within days of arrival. Converted to a hooked Spitfire during the ensuing repairs, it spent the rest of its days with the FAA.

37

[97]: *Spitfire VB R6960 SZ-N, No. 316 Squadron, Hutton Cranswick, December 1942–January 1943. Upper surface camouflage colours: Ocean Grey and Dark Green ('A' pattern); under surface colour: Medium Sea Grey.*

[98]: *R6960 was originally built as a Mk I and was one of the very early cannon-armed Spitfires. In early 1941 its Merlin III engine was replaced by a Merlin 45, which turned it into a Mk VB. Used by No. 91 'Nigeria' Squadron RAF it was given the presentation name 'Nigeria - Owerri Province'. Following service with that unit and then No. 234 Sqn RAF, it was transferred from the latter to No. 316 Sqn, ferried in by Sgt Leon Zygarlicki on 11–13 December 1942. Note how the S looks much paler than Z in the squadron code: it is possible that the latter was retained from No. 234 Sqn's AZ code, only the former being applied anew. On 8 January 1943 Sgt Stefan Sztuka had an accident in R6960 at Hutton Cranswick: while avoiding collision with his leader during a formation take off practice, he struck a pile of frozen snow at the edge of runway, breaking off the port main wheel and leg. Unable to retract the other leg, he made an emergency landing on the starboard wheel, incurring relatively little damage to the aircraft, as shown here. It is noteworthy that the squadron badge had still not been applied by that time, with just the white triangle painted on. The Spitfire resumed service with No. 316 Sqn on 11 February. In March 1943 it was transferred to No. 306 when the units exchanged bases and aircraft. In that unit it was damaged in a landing accident on 26 May 1943 and this terminated its Polish AF connection.*

[99]: A souvenir photo with R6960 in early 1943, with the aircraft letter N in a pale colour (possibly yellow) just visible below the spinner. Posing on the ground, left to right: S/Ldr Marian Trzebiński, unrecognised ground crew, F/O Lech Kondracki (crouching in front) and F/O Józef Dec.

[100]: BL698 was built at the CBAF in early 1942. Following service with a number of units and conversion to LF.VB, it was delivered to No. 316 Sqn during its period of rest at Acklington in November 1943. The unit moved to Woodvale in February 1944, and converted to Mustang IIIs in April. Similar to other Spitfires of No. 316, BL698 then went to No. 63 Sqn (see p. 27), where it was written off in an accident at the end of June. Ground crew member LAC Mendel Lichtensztejn is posing on his bike in front of the Spitfire here.

[101]: Spitfire VB BL698 SZ-A, No. 316 Squadron, Acklington–Woodvale, January–March 1944. Upper surface camouflage colours: Ocean Grey and Dark Green ('A' pattern); under surface colour: Medium Sea Grey.

No. 317 Squadron 'City of Wilno'

Like Nos. 302 and 316 Sqns, No. 317 started conversion to Spitfire Vs in October 1941. It was based at Exeter at the time and was commanded by S/Ldr Henryk Szczęsny. At the beginning of March 1942 S/Ldr Józef Brzeziński took over as the new commander.

On 15 March the squadron suffered the worst loss of aircraft in a single operation in the history of the Polish Air Force. A sudden change of weather and dense mist forced the entire squadron, returning from 'Roadstead 12', to attempt emergency landings in fields. Ten Spitfires were either written off or damaged so heavily that they needed to be sent away for repairs. Considering the circumstances, it was fortunate that only one pilot (S/Ldr Brzeziński) was killed. S/Ldr Piotr Ozyra was appointed the new commander.

On 1 April 1942 No. 317 Squadron moved to Northolt, to join the 1st Wing on intensive operations over the Continent. S/Ldr Ozyra was killed on 29 April during 'Circus 145'. He was succeeded by S/Ldr Stanisław Skalski.

In the first week of September No. 317 Squadron left its Spitfire Vs at Northolt for No. 315, and took over the latter's Mk Vs at Woodvale. On 9 November 1942 Skalski was replaced by S/Ldr Zbigniew Czaykowski at the head of the unit. On 13 February 1943 the squadron moved to Kirton-in-Lindsey. On 15 April S/Ldr Czaykowski was injured in a forced landing caused by an engine failure and hospitalised. S/Ldr Franciszek Kornicki was appointed the new commander. On 29 April the squadron moved to Martlesham Heath.

At the beginning of June 1943 No. 317 Sqn went to Heston, to join the 1 Wing. On 9 June its aircraft were flown to No. 3501 Servicing Unit at Cranfield to be modified to the LF.V standard. The Spitfires were collected a few days later.

On 21 June these were handed over to No. 412 Sqn RCAF at Friston, in exchange for their LR.Vs. This coincided with the squadron's move, together with No. 302 Sqn, to Perranporth in Cornwall, to form the new 3rd Polish Wing. On 19 August both squadrons moved to Fairlop. From this airfield they took part in Operation 'Starkey', which culminated in the feint 'invasion of France' on 9 September. Special markings in form of broad black-and-white bands were applied on the wings of the aircraft for that day.

On 21 September No. 317 moved to rejoin the 1st Polish Wing at Northolt. The unit's LR.Vs were handed over to No. 312 (Czechoslovak) Squadron and the latter's plain Mk Vs were taken over by No. 317 as backup aircraft pending re-equipment with Spitfire LF.IXs. These Spitfire Vs were used by No. 317 to fly a few scrambles and local patrols during the following week, as the pilots and ground crew were getting acquainted with their new mounts. The last Spitfire V sorties were flown by the squadron on 26 September. It seems these aircraft were never repainted in No. 317 markings, but retained their No. 312 Sqn DU codes.

[102]: F/Lt Piotr Ostaszewski on a Spitfire V of No. 317 Sqn. The squadron badge, inherited from the pre-war Wilno-based 151st and 152nd Fighter Flights, which depicted a bird of prey (usually referred to as 'Condor') on a white cross, was initially applied aft of the cockpit on a diamond-shaped background.

[103]: No. 317 Sqn pilots with one of their Spitfire VBs during gunnery practice at Warmwell in early January 1942. Left to right: P/O Roman Hrycak, F/O Witold Łanowski, P/O Zbigniew Borusiewicz, Sgt Jan Malinowski, F/O Stanisław Łukaszewicz, F/O Henryk Malinowski (Engineer Officer), F/O Tadeusz Koc, F/O Lech Xiężopolski, F/O Marian Trzebiński, F/O Ludwik Martel, F/Lt Piotr Ozyra, F/O Tadeusz Szumowski, S/Ldr Henryk Szczęsny, Sgt Marian Domagała, F/O Jerzy Solak, F/O Zbigniew Janicki, P/O Jerzy Zbrożek, F/O Stanisław Bochniak, F/O Tadeusz Kratke, Sgt Piotr Kuryłowicz, P/O Tadeusz Bobola.

[104]: F/O Tadeusz Koc with one of No. 317 Sqn's first Spitfires at Exeter in October 1941 during conversion from Hurricanes (one can be seen in the background). AD308 JH-T was usually flown by F/O Marian Trzebiński. On 15 February 1942 F/Sgt Stanisław Brzeski was scrambled in it and directed to intercept a 'bogey' off the English coast in bad weather. Tragically, after No. 317 Sqn pilots downed it into the sea on Ops Room orders, it was identified as Liberator AM918/G-AGDR, carrying passengers and mail from Cairo! A month later AD308 was among the Spitfires written off in crash-landings after 'Roadstead 12', but F/O Stanisław Łukaszewicz was unhurt.

[105]: Westland repair facility at Ilchester in the last days of January 1942. Each aeroplane has a black board with the serial number and date of arrival attached to the radio mast. Far in the distance W3425 can be seen, with No. 317 Sqn diamond-shaped badge aft of the cockpit. It was damaged in a take-off collision on 18 December 1941. AD313 (ex-JH-D) is in the foreground, with the squadron badge visible on the fuselage spine. The date on its board is 28/1/42. It was probably 'pranged' during the gunnery training at Warmwell in early January. Note how all code letters on these Spitfires are obliterated. BL410 is an exception: it had no codes when damaged in the first days of 1942, just after allocation to No. 412 Sqn RCAF. Repaired by mid-March, it went to No. 317 Sqn in the wake of their ill-fated 'Roadstead 12', becoming the new JH-D.

[106]: 'Roadstead 12' on 15 March 1942 proved that weather was as dangerous an enemy as the Luftwaffe. Following an uneventful mission No. 317 Sqn pilots were unable to land at Predannack or Bolt Head due to sudden onset of ground mist. Only F/O Koc and F/Sgt Brzeski managed to land safely elsewhere (see pp. 48–51). S/Ldr Józef Brzeziński was killed when his BL805 JH-N hit a cliff. The other nine pilots survived their crash landings, four of them suffering injuries. Altogether five Spitfires were written-off and five seriously damaged. This is the crashsite near Prawle, where F/O Jerzy Mencel's AD350 JH-F and Sgt Władysław Grobelny's AD351 JH-L collided during forced landings. Mencel suffered injuries to his face and arm, but Grobelny was unhurt.

[107]: Cpl Wincenty Szatkowski in front of AA762 JH-W, one of five Spitfires that survived 15 March 1942 by not participating in 'Roadstead 12'. In 1941–1942 white swastika victory markings were painted on No. 317 Sqn Spitfire noses. It seems that in this case these symbols denoted the two 109s credited to F/Sgt Michał Maciejowski on 30 December 1941 while flying AA762. This Spitfire was unusual in that the Polish AF marking was applied without the word 'POLAND' beneath and positioned immediately aft of the propeller, even further forward than the position typical for No. 303 Sqn at the time (see vol. 1). AA762 was subsequently written off in No. 315 Sqn use (see p. 5).

[108]: AD269 JH-B was another Spitfire VB delivered in 1941 that did not fly on 15 March 1942 and survived until transfer to No. 315 Sqn in September. It provides a good example of the standard layout of markings on the rear fuselage. On 18 December 1941 P/O Zbigniew Janicki was credited with a Messerschmitt 109 destroyed while flying it, so it may have had a white swastika on the nose.

[109]: BL860 JH-T was a good example of another common motif in No. 317 Sqn: many Spitfires displayed personal names applied in ornamental style forward of or below the windscreen (usually on both sides of the fuselage). In this case, Hala was the first name of the pre-war girlfriend of the usual pilot, P/O Stanisław Bochniak. He is shown here in the cockpit with Cpl Władysław Brzózkiewicz beside.

[110]: EN916 JH-J was the personal mount of W/Cdr Stefan Janus, Northolt Wing Leader. During late June 1942 W/Cdr Janus visited No. 315 Sqn at Woodvale. By the time he left, the latter unit's personnel covered his Spitfire VB with chalked messages for their Northolt friends. This photo was taken upon arrival at the destination, where the 'air mail' was studied thoroughly. As explained in vol. 1, the position of the Polish AF marking below the first section of exhausts was standard for No. 303 Sqn, who had maintained the WingCo's Spitfire during May and early June.

[111]: AB215 had succeeded W3618 (see pp. 14–15) as PK-J with No. 315 Sqn at Woodvale in early June 1942, and in early September it went to No. 317 when the squadrons exchanged bases and aircraft. It is shown as JH-J in the autumn of 1942, the code letter still in No. 315's style with the horizontal bar. Note the absence of the Polish AF marking on the nose. The paint erosion on the back of the propeller blade is also noteworthy.

[112]: By February 1943, AB215 had been completely repainted, with the JH-J now in standard style of No. 317 Sqn. The Polish marking had been applied in that squadron's typical form, with 'POLAND' beneath the square. During 1942 it became standard to apply No. 317 Sqn badge below the windscreen rather than aft of the cockpit. The paint wear on the propeller blade seems as bad as in the earlier shot, if not worse.

Polish Wings

[113]: BM597 was another Spitfire VB transferred from No. 315 (see p. 4) to No 317 Sqn at Woodvale in early September 1942. This view shows the oversize underwing roundels seen on Spitfires that had these insignia changed while with by No. 315 Sqn (see AD262 on p. 17).

[114]: This side view of BM597 in service with No. 317 in late 1942 shows a dark patch below the windscreen. The irregular patch of dark colour surrounds a slightly paler diamond shape, the size of which is roughly the same as that of the early squadron badge. Unfortunately, no photos are known to show the squadron badge or any other emblem in that place on BM597. Posing with the Spitfire are, left to right: Cpl Stanisław Krysztofiak, unidentified, LAC Władysław Wodczyński, Cpl Edward Ancuta, unidentified.

[115, 116]: On the port side, the squadron code letters JH were invariably applied near the cockpit. On the starboard side, however, the arrangement of the codes seems to have been altered in 1943, probably following the exchange of aircraft with No. 412 Sqn in June. Until that time the JH code was applied near the cockpit, as shown on W3207 JH-M at Kirton-in-Lindsey in February 1943 [115]. Subsequently the squadron letters were applied near the tail, as shown on another Mk VB coded JH-M, believed to be EP411, in the summer of 1943 at RAF Perranporth [116].

[117]: *Few photographs of No. 317 Sqn Spitfire VCs are known. This clipped-wing Mk VC being serviced at RAF Perranporth in the summer of 1943 is probably EE717 JH-J.*

[118]: *S/Ldr Franciszek Kornicki with a WAAF by a Spitfire VC (probably EE715 JH-N) of No. 317 Sqn on 9 September 1943, the final day of Operation 'Starkey'. Note the quick recognition markings introduced for the feint 'invasion' that day: broad black and white bands on outer wings.*

[119, 120]: *Spitfire LR.VB AB198 JH-T with No. 317 Sqn ground crew at Perranporth in the summer of 1943.*

[121]: *The same Spitfire upon transfer to No. 312 (Czechoslovak) Sqn in late September, with F/O Antonín Dvořák in the cockpit. Note the new round rear-view mirror, still in its black primer.*

[122]: *CBAF-built AD350, one of the first Spitfire VBs delivered to No. 317 Sqn in October 1941, was selected by S/Ldr Henryk 'Hesio' Szczęsny as his personal mount, adorned with his nickname under the cockpit and two white swastikas on the nose, probably denoting his two shared 'kills' scored with No. 317 (though he had scored many more victories by that time) in addition to the Polish AF square on the nose and the squadron badge aft of the cockpit. In early January 1942 S/Ldr Szczęsny chose BL543 as his new JH-S and AD350 was re-coded JH-F. It was written off on 15 March 1942 (see p. 42).*

(see p. 42)

[123]: *S/Ldr Szczęsny (centre, with the decorations pinned on) with No. 317 Sqn ground crew by AD350 JH-S in November 1941. Directly to the left of his is Cpl Antoni Musielak with his unmistakable black moustache. Cpl Władysław Kembłowski is standing third left (greyhaired). Note the paint now peeling both on the wing and near the fuselage roundel.*

[124, 125]: *Two images of 'Hesio' Szczęsny in his Spitfire. Note the badge of No. 317 Sqn on the spine of the Spitfire, and that of No. 74 'Tiger' Sqn RAF sewn-on at the bottom of his 'Mae-West'. The name 'Hesio' on the side of the aircraft seems complete in photo [125], but in [124] it has a gap where paint has peeled off. Careful inspection of [125] shows that the original print has been retouched.*

[125]

[127]

[126]

[128]

[126]: An unrecognised mechanic by the side of AD350 while it was still in pristine condition. This style of 'Hesio' was very similar to that of 'Hala' on BL860 (see p. 42).

[127]: F/O Stanisław Łukaszewicz (in the cockpit) and AC1 Jan Awdziejew with the next 'Hesio', BL543 JH-S. Note the different style of the personal name, similar to that of 'Sheila' (see p. 49). S/Ldr Szczęsny left No. 317 Sqn on 1 March and his BL543 was written-off two weeks later when F/O Lech Xiężopolski crash-landed in it at the end of 'Roadstead 12'.

[128]: Spitfire VB AD350 JH-S, No. 317 Squadron, Exeter, October 1941–January 1942. Upper surface camouflage colours: Ocean Grey and Dark Green ('A' pattern); under surface colour: Medium Sea Grey.

131

132

133

129

130

[129, 130]: W3424 was a fairly early Spitfire VB from Supermarine production, delivered originally to No. 616 Sqn in July 1941. Following an accident and repairs it went to No. 317, becoming the regular mount of Sgt (then F/Sgt) Stanisław Brzeski in late 1941. On 6 December 1941 he used W3424 to claim a Junkers 88 destroyed over Plymouth Sound. It was probably this victory that was marked by a white swastika on the nose of the Spitfire. Posing in [130] are, left to right: Cpl Edward Ancuta, LAC Stefan Kowalski and AC1 Jan Awdziejew.

[131–133]: F/Sgt Mirosław Maciejowski [131] and F/O Witold Łanowski [132–133] in an early Supermarine-built Spitfire, possibly also W3424 before the name 'Sheila' was applied. Note the Supermarine style of the warning note inside the door (in three horizontal lines on the middle section) and the white stencilled instruction on the radio hatch, on top of the roundel.

[134]: *Spitfire VB W3424 JH-Q, No. 317 Squadron, Exeter-Northolt, November 1941–May 1942. Upper surface camouflage colours: Ocean Grey and Dark Green ('A' pattern); under surface colour: Medium Sea Grey.*

[135]: *A vic of No. 317 Sqn Spitfire VBs in early 1942: W3970 JH-Y in the lead (see pp. 50–51) with W3424 JH-Q and AA758 JH-V on the wings.*

[136]: *W3424 displayed a personal name, 'Sheila', below the windscreen. Sgt Stanisław Brzeski, shown here, was the usual pilot in late 1941 and from mid-March 1942 on. Flying this Spitfire during 'Roadstead 12' on 15 March, he was one of just two pilots who landed safely in the appalling conditions. Other pilots scored in W3424 in April 1942: F/O Tadeusz Kurniega an FW 190 shared damaged on the 26th and F/O Przesław Sadowski a 190 probably destroyed on the 27th. On 3 May, however, the undercarriage was damaged during take-off by Sgt Piotr Kuryłłowicz and W3424 was written-off in the crash-landing (the pilot was unhurt).*

49

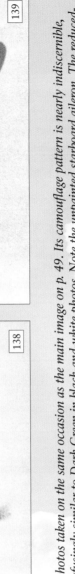

[137–139, 141–144]: Spitfire VB W3970 JH-Y in a series of air-to-air photos taken on the same occasion as the main image on p. 49. Its camouflage pattern is nearly indiscernible, because the hue in place of Ocean Grey is much darker, and appears confusingly similar to Dark Green in black-and-white photos. Note the unpainted starboard aileron. The reduced-size roundels are mysterious. Such markings were introduced in February 1942 on all-black night-flying Spitfires of two RAF squadrons, Nos. 65 and 111. However, W3970 was not used by either of these, serving with No. 317 Sqn since delivery from Supermarine production, via No. 39 MU, in October 1941, until June 1942. Its roundels may have been repainted during repairs following damage in ground collision, when it was hit by No. 307 Sqn Beaufighter T3046 on 21 December 1941. Between November 1941 and early April 1942 W3970 was often flown by F/O Tadeusz Koc. On 8 November he used it when he was credited with a Messerschmitt 109 probably destroyed. On 15 March 1942 he managed to land W3970 safely during the disastrous 'Roadstead 12', one of only two pilots to avoid a crash-landing. It is not impossible that the undersize roundels on the Spitfire were a 'private venture' of this pilot, as his next regular mount with No. 317 Sqn, BL563 JH-M, also featured such markings. On 30 June W3970 was heavily damaged in a landing accident of F/O Zbigniew Janicki at Croydon. Its subsequent career included a few months with No. 302 Sqn in the spring of 1943.

[140]: Spitfire VB W3970 JH-Y, No. 317 Squadron, Exeter–Northolt, January–April 1942. Upper surface camouflage colours: unspecified dark grey in place of Ocean Grey and Dark Green ('A' pattern); under surface colour: Medium Sea Grey.

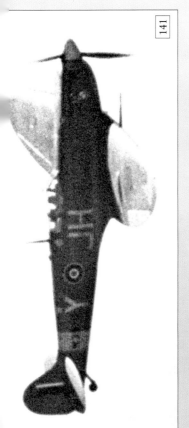

[145]: CBAF-built BL563 was delivered brand new to No. 317 Sqn in early January 1942 and received the code JH-M. It is not clear when and by whom the small size roundels were applied. Between mid-April and early June 1942 it was usually flown by F/O Tadeusz Koc who scored three victories in it: a Focke-Wulf 190 destroyed on 28 April and a 190 destroyed plus another probably destroyed the following day. After Koc left No. 317 in June, the Spitfire was often flown by F/O Stanisław Łukaszewicz, who claimed an FW 190 damaged on 15 July. During its time with No. 317 Sqn the Spitfire was also flown by a number of other notable pilots, including F/Sgts Brzeski, Maciejowski and Sztramko, as well as S/Ldr Nowierski from the Northolt Wing HQ. Researching the history of the aeroplane with No. 317 is difficult because it was often confused in documents with BL543 (JH-S 'Hesio'), used by the unit between January and March 1942.

146

147

[146]: CBAF-built BL627 was another Mk VB paid for by the Prins Bernard Fond (see p. 34), Wonosobo being a town on Java. It was delivered brand new to No. 317 Sqn in mid-March 1942, in the wake of the 'Roadstead 12' disaster. This photo was taken soon after No. 317 Sqn moved to Northolt in early April 1942. The Spitfire displayed a standard set of regulation markings, including the Polish AF square and 'POLAND' on the nose. Note the absence of the squadron badge. On 25 April F/O Stanisław Bochniak flew BL627 when he participated in the downing of an FW 190 together with F/O Tadeusz Koc and F/O Zygmunt Słomski, but for unclear reasons the victory was eventually only credited to the latter two pilots.

[147]: A group of ground crew photographed on the same occasion. AC1 Jan Awdziejew is at the top, leaning on the fuselage. AC1 Gerard Stomski is seated on the wing root. LAC Władysław Wodczyński holds his hand on the cannon. AC1 Stanisław Byszyński is standing directly below the Polish AF square.

[148]: *Spitfire VB BL627 JH-H, No. 317 Squadron, Exeter–Northolt, March–April 1942. Upper surface camouflage colours: Ocean Grey and Dark Green ('A' pattern); under surface colour: Medium Sea Grey.*

[149]: *BL627 JH-H 'Wonosobo' photographed at Northolt after the new bulged Malcolm hood was fitted over the cockpit. Note that its framing is still unpainted. AC1 Wincenty Manicki is at far left.*

[150]: *P/O Stanisław Elmerych, the usual pilot of BL627 until the first week of May, photographed with it. The photo was taken after some re-spraying of the nose: the edges of the Polish AF square and the bottom of the letters PO are partly obliterated. Note the '12 V' voltage mark, probably in yellow, near the start-up socket.*

53

[151]: F/O Tadeusz Kratke was the usual pilot of BL627 JH-H during May, June and July 1942. On 24 July he flew it when he strafed Messerschmitt 109s parked at the Luftwaffe airfield at Offrethun in France, claiming damage to at least three of these. Exactly one week later, on the 31st, Kratke was shot down by Focke-Wulfs in this Spitfire. He baled out into the Channel about 30 miles off the British coast and was rescued after two hours in the dinghy.

[152, 153]: These photos were taken in July 1942, after introduction of the altered form of roundels. By that time the Spitfire displayed No. 317 Sqn badge in the new style: below the windscreen and without the diamond-shaped background.

[154]: At some point the presentation name 'Wonosobo' was replaced on both sides of the Spitfire by an ornamentally applied word 'Mała', probably in yellow. 'Mała' is a feminine form of 'Little One', probably referring to a girl here. The removal of a presentation name was not a usual occurrence, but in this case it can probably be explained by an unfortunate linguistic coincidence. While most of the Dutch East Indies presentation names simply sounded exotic, occasionally they resembled Polish words (as already mentioned on p. 34). As regards 'Wonosobo', if it is read as two words, it sounds rather rude in Polish, even if it is not a phrase that would normally be used. 'Won' is a very impolite way of asking somebody to leave immediately, while 'osobo' is a vocative form of the word for 'a person' in Polish. Put together they form a strange but unequivocal phrase, something like 'Get lost, you person'.

[155]: Spitfire VB BL627 JH-H, No. 317 Squadron, Northolt, July 1942. Upper surface camouflage colours: Ocean Grey and Dark Green ('A' pattern); under surface colour: Medium Sea Grey.

[156]: *Spitfire VB AD262 JH-Z, No. 317 Squadron, Woodvale–Kirton-in-Lindsey, September 1942–March 1943. Upper surface camouflage colours: Ocean Grey and Dark Green ('A' pattern); under surface colour: Medium Sea Grey.*

[157, 158]: *AD262 had been used by No. 315 Sqn (see pp. 16–17). In early September 1942 it was taken over by No. 317 Sqn at Woodvale. By the time these photos were taken there in late 1942 or early 1943 the Spitfire must have undergone a partial repaint. There are no clear signs of obliterating previous codes, so the part of the fuselage from the cockpit door aft was probably given a new finish. The nose section was most probably not repainted, as the Polish AF square is still in No. 315 style, without 'POLAND' below it. Note also AB914 JH-S in the background. It had previously been used by No. 315 Sqn as PK-Z and then PK-R. Although it had left the CBAF with the Rotol propeller, it was refitted with a de Havilland one during repairs following an accident.*

[159]: Sgt Ryszard Lewczyński in the cockpit of AD262, assisted by LACs Józef Waśniowski (left) and Wiktor Piwowarczyk. The cartoon dwarf motif was positioned in the middle of the panel below the windscreen, and it may well have dated back to No. 315 Sqn. The badge of No. 317 seems to have been a subsequent addition to an already applied personal emblem. The significance of the name 'Teofilek' ('Little Teofil') is not known.

[160]: As far as can be ascertained, the exiled Polish AF had only one fighter pilot with this first name: F/O Teofil Szymankiewicz, who flew with No. 317 Sqn between April and December 1942. Unfortunately, virtually no flying records of the unit from late 1942 survive and it has not been possible to verify if he flew AD262 JH-Z. As far as could be ascertained, no ground crew member whose first name was Teofil served with Nos. 317 or 315 Sqns during 1941–1943.

[161]: At least one more Spitfire VB transferred from No. 315 to No 317 Sqn, W3507 JH-Q, featured a cartoon emblem that may have depicted a dwarf (with the name 'Dopey' added below). It is, of course, certain that another dwarf motif had been applied on a Spitfire of No. 315 Sqn earlier on (see pp. 9–11). There are unconfirmed accounts of dwarf images being applied on seven (naturally!) Spitfires of that unit. Whether that was true and how many made it to No. 317 Sqn (and whether the Snow White was there as well!) is a potential subject for further research.

[162]: AB241 JH-E photographed at Woodvale soon after transfer to No. 317 Sqn at Woodvale in September 1942, before it was repainted in this unit. The Supermarine-built Spitfire VB had been delivered brand new to No. 315 Sqn at Northolt in December 1941. It moved with the squadron to Woodvale in April 1942 and on 3 May F/O Konrad Stembrowicz flew it when he was credited with a Junkers 88 shared damaged.

[163, 164, 166]: Three photos of the Spitfire at Woodvale in early 1943. At the time it displayed the squadron badge below the windscreen, and the name 'Zosia' (Sophie) forward of the badge on both sides of the fuselage. Although this is a girl's name, in this case it presumably referred to F/O Ludwik Martel, who often flew this Spitfire, and who had been known as 'Zosia' or 'Zośka' (another form of Sophie in Polish) since before the war. It seems that by the time of these photos the Ocean Grey areas had been resprayed with a non-standard pale grey, following the prescribed pattern only roughly. The code letters and roundel must have been masked off for this, which resulted in an uneven dark outline. The rear fuselage seems to have been repainted in a particularly careless manner. The serial number was re-applied in small characters on the Sky band with a hyphen between the letters and the digits. The under surfaces were also repainted, obliterating the aircraft letter on the bottom of the engine cowling. Martel left No. 317 Sqn in mid-February 1943 to go to Africa (see p. 71) and two months later the Spitfire was sent away for a major overhaul, which terminated its association with Polish squadrons.

164

162

58

163

[165]: *Spitfire VB AB241 JH-E, No. 317 Squadron, Woodvale–Kirton-in-Lindsey, February–April 1943. Upper surface camouflage colours: Ocean Grey and Dark Green (approx. 'A' pattern); under surface colour: Medium Sea Grey.*

[167]: *Spitfire VC EE714 JH-P, No. 317 Squadron, Perranporth–Fairlop, June–August 1943. Upper surface camouflage colours: Ocean Grey and Dark Green ('A' pattern); under surface colour: Medium Sea Grey.*

[168, 169]: *Two souvenir photos of an anonymous mechanic with a clipped-wing Spitfire VC coded JH-P at RAF Perranporth in the summer of 1943. The aircraft is believed to be EE714, one of a number of Mk VCs taken over from No. 412 Sqn RCAF on 21 June 1943. Note the absence of the blunt protrusion on the leading edge just outboard of the cannon, normally seen on the C wing. This means that it had undergone the Modification 820 ('To remove the outboard cannon front mount casting'). This modification was also seen on other Mk VCs of No. 317 Sqn. Another non-standard item seen on many Spitfires of the unit at the time was the rear-view mirror fitted inside the windscreen rather than on top of it.*

Non-Polish squadrons of Fighter Command

Although the exiled Polish Air Force had seven day fighter squadrons at the time when Spitfire V entered service, quite a lot of Polish pilots flew the variant with non-Polish squadrons as well.

In fact even before Polish units started receiving Mk Vs a few Polish pilots flew these with Nos. 72, 74, and 92 Squadrons. Then, between late 1941 and 1943, Poles flew Spitfire Vs with the following RAF and allied fighter squadrons in Britain: Nos. 19, 41, 54, 64, 65, 66, 72, 81, 124, 129, 130, 132, 164, 165, 222, 234, 242, 243, 310 (Czechoslovak), 401 RCAF, 403 RCAF, 453 RAAF, 501, 504, 602, 603, 610 and 611.

Notably, in 1942, No. 222 Squadron was commanded by S/Ldr Jerzy Jankiewicz – the first Polish officer to hold this post with an RAF squadron.

[170]: Early Spitfire Vs of No. 72 'Basutoland' Squadron in late July or August 1941 at Biggin Hill. This was one of the so-called 'Gift Squadrons', their aircraft funded by wealthy individuals or groups of people from certain countries, in this case Basuto (now Lesotho), in Africa (hence the name on W3380 RN-J in the foregorund). At the time No. 72 Sqn had two Polish pilots: F/Lt Kazimierz Kosiński and F/O Henryk Skalski (not to be confused with the famous ace Stanisław Skalski!). When this photo was taken the Spitfires were still in the Temperate Land scheme (Dark Earth/Dark Green) on top with Sky undersides. Second in this line-up is probably P8783 RN-N, usually flown by F/Lt Dennis Secretan. F/O H. Skalski flew it on 21 August in this guise. The Spitfire was used by F/Lt Kosiński on 1 October, when he was credited with a Messerschmitt 109 destroyed and another probably destroyed. By that time, however, the colours had been changed to the grey-and-green Day Fighter scheme.

[171]: Spitfire VB BL469 FL-V of No. 81 Squadron was flown by no less than three Polish pilots with the unit during April 1942: F/O Zbigniew Zarębski, P/O Adam Damm, and Sgt Tadeusz Bubes. It was in standard Day Fighter scheme with regulation markings and codes.

[172]: W3114 was an early Spitfire VA, built in May 1941. By early 1942 the cannon-less variant was obsolete against Luftwaffe fighters. The Spitfire was allocated to No. 164 Sqn at Skaebrae in the Orkneys where, between May and July, it was repeatedly flown by F/O Ignacy Olszewski and P/O Stanisław Blok. The Poles flew W3114 with both early, and late style roundels and fin flashes (the latter shown here) as the change of markings took place during that period. No. 164 was another 'Gift Squadron', its aircraft funded by the Argentine Patriotic Fund, which contributed 100,000 pound sterling, hence the inscription 'ARGENTINE (BRITISH)' on the cowling.

173

[173]: *A trio of No. 222 Sqn Spitfires in flight. BL312 ZD-P and AB867 ZD-E appear to be finished in quite standard Day Fighter scheme of Ocean Grey and Dark Green. The Dark Green on AD233 ZD-F also looks rather standard, but most of its grey is much darker, this being particularly obvious on the rear fuselage and rudder. Note the presentation name WEST BORNEO I stencilled on forward fuselage. The bluish item below the windscreen is the Squadron Leader pennant, as this was the personal aircraft of No. 222 Sqn commander, S/Ldr Richard Milne at the time of these photos.*

174

[174]: *When S/Ldr Jerzy Jankiewicz took over the unit in May 1942 (the first Polish pilot to command an RAF squadron), he also inherited AD233 ZD-F as his personal mount. He was killed in it during 'Rodeo 51' over Gravelines on 25 May 1942.*

[175]: *AD233 had originally been delivered to the RAF in September 1941 in the Temperate Land scheme (Dark Earth and Dark Green), with black spinner and no Sky band on the rear fuselage. Upon delivery, No. 37 MU changed its finish according to the regulations of the time: Dark Earth areas were resprayed grey (obliterating the presentation name on the starboard side in the process) and the quick recognition markings in Sky were applied on the spinner and fuselage. The dark grey paint used on this Spitfire was certainly not the regulation Ocean Grey. During the application of the Sky band (or possibly during repairs after the Spitfire was damaged in late 1941) the serial number was obliterated and reapplied in small characters at the top of the fin. The top engine cowling, both ailerons, and the starboard wingtip must have been replacement items as they seem to feature the correct Ocean Grey.*

175

[176]: Mk VB AR382 was used by No. 234 Sqn as AZ-V, featuring the personal emblem of F/Lt Derek Glaser near the cockpit. This photo was taken after the British national markings were changed in late June, but otherwise the Spitfire must have looked the same when flown repeatedly by F/O Bronisław Wydrowski in May and June 1942. Notably, AR382 was subsequently used by No. 316 Sqn and lost in a fatal accident in April 1943 (see p. 95).

[177]: Sgt Roman Dąbrowski flew BL328 SN-P in No. 243 Sqn during a scramble from Ouston very late in the evening on 31 July 1942. So late, in fact, that the mission was not included in the July pages of the Squadron Operations Record Book. Perhaps as an example of English sense of humour rather than clerical error, the operation was then entered at the beginning of the August chapter of that document, under the date of '32.7.42'!

[178]: This photo shows at least two Spitfires flown by Polish pilots with No. 19 Sqn. QV-S is EP465, used by P/O Ludwik Kraszewski during March 1943. QV-M in the foreground is either EP445 or EP447. The former was used by P/O Kraszewski in March 1943 and by Sgt Wiktor Ciechanowicz in February of that year. EP447, on the other hand, was flown by F/O Tadeusz Bobola repeatedly in December 1942 and January 1943.

[179]: BL267 PJ-B is a peculiar case as it was a No. 130 Squadron Spitfire flown by a Polish pilot who was at the time serving with No. 315 Squadron of the Polish AF. When the latter unit replaced No. 130 at RAF Ballyhalbert in the summer of 1943, BL267 was left behind, unserviceable at the time, remaining on charge of No. 130 Sqn. Following repairs, F/Sgt Stanisław Będkowski test flew the Spitfire on 17 August, still as PJ-B. It was then ferried away to No. 349 (Belgian) Squadron RAF.

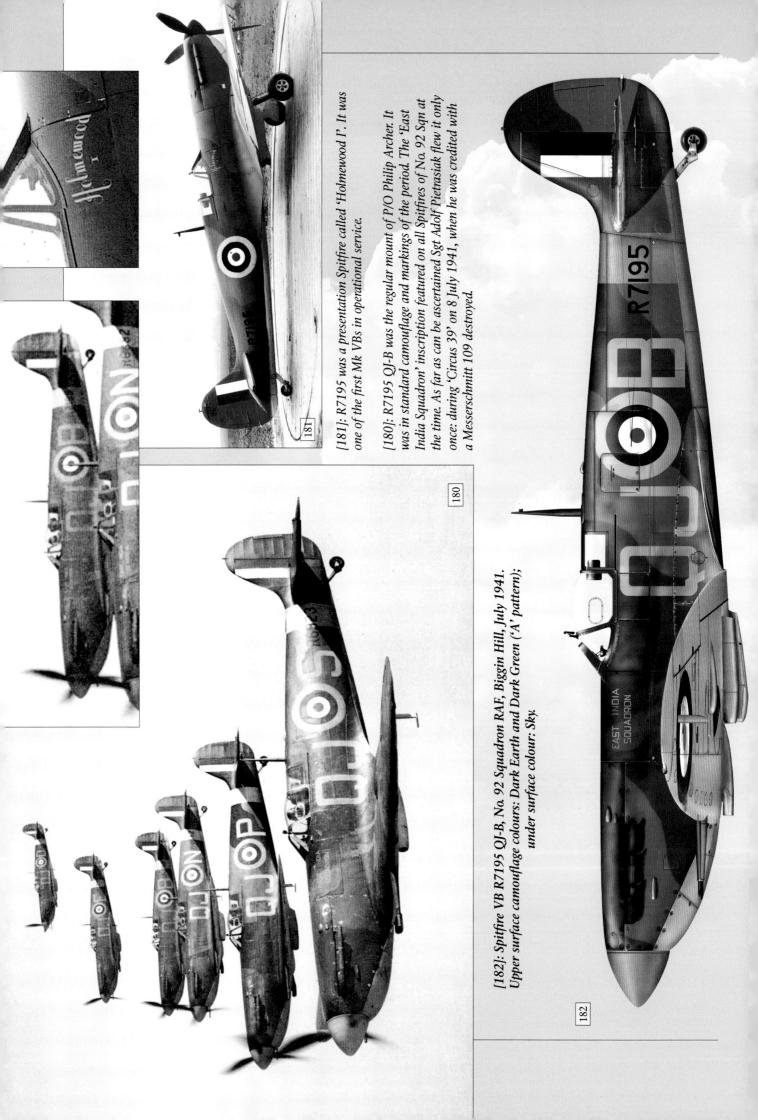

[181]: R7195 was a presentation Spitfire called 'Holmewood I'. It was one of the first Mk VBs in operational service.

[180]: R7195 QJ-B was the regular mount of P/O Philip Archer. It was in standard camouflage and markings of the period. The 'East India Squadron' inscription featured on all Spitfires of No. 92 Sqn at the time. As far as can be ascertained Sgt Adolf Pietrasiak flew it only once: during 'Circus 39' on 8 July 1941, when he was credited with a Messerschmitt 109 destroyed.

[182]: Spitfire VB R7195 QJ-B, No. 92 Squadron RAF, Biggin Hill, July 1941. Upper surface camouflage colours: Dark Earth and Dark Green ('A' pattern); under surface colour: Sky.

183

184

[183]: Spitfire VB AD502 XT-Z, No. 603 Squadron RAF, Peterhead, March 1942. Upper surface camouflage colours: Ocean Grey and Dark Green ('A' pattern); under surface colour: Medium Sea Grey.

[184]: During March 1942 F/O Ignacy Olszewski and P/O Stanisław Błok flew Spitfire VB AD502 XT-Z during their posting to No. 603 Squadron at RAF Peterhead. The aeroplane had been delivered to the unit brand new in October 1941. For some reason the serial number was overpainted, leaving a prominent patch of slightly different tones under the code letter T, and re-applied in small characters below the tailplane. In April 1942 No. 603 Sqn went to Malta, the Polish pilots were re-posted to No. 54 Sqn, and AD502 was transferred to the Norwegian No. 332 Sqn.

Non-operational units

Polish pilots under training and instructors flew Spitfire Vs with the Polish Fighter School (*Polska Szkoła Myśliwska*) that operated alongside No. 58 OTU at Grangemouth until October 1943, and then alongside No. 61 OTU at Rednal, where it continued to exist until the end of the war. Poles also flew the variant as instructors with No. 53 OTU at Kirton-in-Lindsey and Hibaldstow.

Polish pilots also flew Spitfire Vs with target towing and other non-operational units.

Polish ferry pilots flew these aircraft between RAF and allied units.

Polish test pilots flew Mk Vs in trials at the RAE Farnborough and the AAEE Boscombe Down. They also performed post-overhaul test flights in these aircraft at various maintenance units and facilities.

[185]: A group of instructors and pupil pilots of the Polish Fighter School at No. 61 OTU at Rednal in the summer of 1944. The Spitfire is a Mk VA converted from an early Mk IA, L1031 (the serial number can be discerned at the top of the fin). 'Double-U' was one of several code letter combinations used by that OTU.

[186]: This Mk VB HX-R of No. 61 OTU, also used in training of Polish fighter pilots, is believed to be EP504 (the serial number can just be made out at the base of the fin, in pale characters – probably white or Sky). EP504 had seen service with Nos. 303 and 315 Sqns before being allocated to No. 61 OTU.

[187]: Mk VA W3112 was repeatedly flown by S/Ldr Janusz Żurakowski during his training at the Empire Test Pilots School in 1944.

[188, 189]: *On 25–26 May 1941 F/O Stanisław Marcisz of No. 10 (Polish) Ferry Flight ferried R7264 from No. 38 MU at Llandow to No. 54 Sqn RAF at Hornchurch. This was a presentation aircraft, adorned with the Welsh name of the County of Breconshire, 'Brycheiniog', applied in ornamental style near the cockpit. The photos show it in factory-fresh condition. By the time it was ferried by Marcisz the spinner had been repainted Sky and a band in the same colour was applied on the rear fuselage.*

[190]: *AB488 was an early Mk VC built by Supermarine. On 25 January 1942 Polish 'Spitfire girl' 1st/Off Anna Leska ferried it from the factory airfield at Eastleigh to White Waltham, this being the first leg of its delivery from the makers to No. 9 MU.*

[191]: *1st/Off Anna Leska of No. 15 FP ATA in the cockpit of a Spitfire V at about the same time. The cockpit construction number shown on the fuselage side, CBAF/1119, suggest this might be Mk VB AB968, in which she made a 30-minute local flight from Hamble on 28 February 1942 (presumably a failed delivery flight, possibly due to weather).*

[192]: *W3632 was an early Mk VB used by the 52nd Fighter Group USAAF in Britain until late 1942: first by the 5th Fighter Squadron (coded VF-Z) and then by the 2nd FS (QP-Z). The Spitfire had been funded by the Persian Gulf Fighter Fund and originally called 'Bahrain'. By the time this photo was taken the presentation name (originally applied in both Latin and Arabic characters) was replaced by the word 'Snake' and a relevant image below. When the American units departed for the Operation 'Torch' in North Africa, their Spitfires were distributed to other establishments. W3632 was ferried by Polish ATA pilot 1st/Off Ludwik Tokarczyk from Goxhill to Atcham on 8 December 1942, probably still in these markings. It was then used by the 109th Reconnaissance Squadron of the 67th Reconnaissance Group USAAF.*

[193]: *Spitfire VB AA937 AF-0, Air Fighting Development Unit, Duxford, January–February 1943. Upper surface camouflage colours: Ocean Grey and Dark Green ('A' pattern); under surface colour: Medium Sea Grey.*

193

194

196

197

195

[194–197]: AA937 was a Supermarine-built Mk VB allocated for trials in late 1942 and flown by the Air Fighting Development Unit at Duxford from January 1943. Wooden plugs replaced standard wing tips for trials, note the absence of wing tip lights. F/Lt Jerzy Solak flew it repeatedly there in late January and early February. Although used in trials, the Spitfire was in perfectly standard Day Fighter colour scheme with regulation markings.

69

[198]: Spitfire VA R7302 HX-N of No. 61 OTU following a landing accident of Sgt Andrzej Dąbrowski on 2 June 1944. It was caused by an engine failure: the undamaged upper blade shows that the propeller was not rotating on touch down. Note the reinforcing strakes over the wheel wells and the under-wing carrier for practice bombs.

[199]: Spitfire VA R7302 HX-N, No. 61 Operational Training Unit, Rednal, June 1944. Upper surface camouflage colours: Ocean Grey and Dark Green ('A' pattern); under surface colour: Medium Sea Grey.

[200]: Unusually for such an early Mk V (R7302 was built in April 1941) it features the late-style tailplane/elevator with enlarged horn balance, presumably fitted during repairs following an accident it suffered in August 1943, while in use with No. 14 Group Communications Flight.

Fighter units in the Mediterranean 1943

The Polish flight, known officially as the Polish Combat Team or Polish Fighting Team, entered history as 'Skalski's Circus'. Although it achieved its great successes on Spitfire IXs, it was initially equipped with tropicalised Mk Vs, as was the entire No. 145 Sqn, to which it was attached as the 'C' Flight in the spring of 1943. W/Cdr Tadeusz Rolski was in command of the team and S/Ldr Stanisław Skalski was the Squadron Leader Flying.

First Spitfire Vs were received on 11 March, but it took until the 16th before the flight had its full number of aircraft. Due to the nature of ground military operations in the Western Desert at the time, flying units used makeshift airfields near the front line and moved as the ground troops advanced. Initially the unit was based at Bu Grara. Some operations on Mk Vs were flown from that airfield during late March, but before the end of the month the flight re-equipped with Spitfire IXs (see 'Polish Wings 13').

Following the Allied victory in Africa, three pilots of the Polish Combat Team became flight and squadron commanders with RAF squadrons: Nos. 43 (S/Ldr Eugeniusz Horbaczewski), 152 (F/Lt Władysław Drecki) and 601 (S/Ldr Stanisław Skalski).

[201]: W/O Bronisław Malinowski in front of a tropicalised Spitfire V with the aircraft letter E on the front cowling. No photos of 'Skalski's Circus' Spitfire Vs have surfaced so far. These would have been easy to spot as the flight used individual aircraft numbers instead of letters alongside the ZX codes of No. 145 Sqn.

[202]: Mk VB ES252 ZX-E, the mount of S/Ldr Lance Wade, OC No. 145 Squadron, provided backdrop for the photographs of the Polish pilots shown here. It was in the Desert scheme of Dark Earth and Middle Stone, with the under surfaces in Light Mediterranean Blue or Azure. The spinner was red as the Allied quick recognition marking in the Mediterranean theatre.

[203]: Pilots of the team with ZX-E, left to right: F/O Kazimierz Sporny, F/O Ludwik Martel, F/Lt Karol Pniak, F/O Władysław Drecki, F/Lt Eugeniusz Horbaczewski, W/O Władysław Majchrzyk, P/O Jan Kowalski (crouching), F/Sgt Marcin Machowiak, W/O Bronisław Malinowski (seated on the ground), F/Sgt Kazimierz Sztramko, F/Lt Wacław Król, S/Ldr Stanisław Skalski, W/O Mieczysław Popek (on the wing).

[204, 205]: *After the 'Circus' was disbanded F/Lt Maciej Drecki continued to fly with No. 145 from Malta and then from Sicily, including at least three sorties in Mk VC EE781 ZX-A shown here. In Africa, No. 145 Sqn Spitfires were mostly finished in the Desert Scheme of Dark Earth and Middle Stone. However, in the colour photo (taken in Sicily) the engine cowling of ZX-A seems to be finished in Dark Earth and Dark Green. It may have been a replacement component cannibalised from a Malta-based Mk V finished in the Temperate Land scheme.*

[206]: *No. 43 Squadron Spitfire Vs at a dusty airfield, probably Tusciano near Salerno, in September 1943. JK539 FT-C is shown to advantage. It was flown by F/Lt Eugeniusz Horbaczewski in the first days of August 1943 from Pachino airfield in southern Sicily. Although the Spitfire behind JK539 is obscured by clouds of dust, the aircraft letter G can be seen. This is believed to be Mk VC MA345 FT-G, Horbaczewski's regular mount between July and September (he commanded the 'A' Flight and then the whole squadron). On 27 July he flew it when he shared in the destruction of a Messerschmitt 109, which he never claimed, in favour of the other two pilots. It seems that at least until the allied landings on Italian mainland the Spitfires continued to be finished in the Desert scheme, with under surfaces in either Azure or Light Mediterranean Blue.*

[207]: Tropicalised Mk VB EP689 UF-X was used by No. 601 Squadron in 1943 when the unit was commanded by S/Ldr Stanisław Skalski. He flew it on his first sortie with No. 601, on 5 July, before he assumed command of the squadron. The aircraft was in the Desert scheme. The red spinner was a quick recognition marking of allied fighters in the theatre. The squadron badge was applied in a white disc at the top of the fin. The dark codes (shown in Roundel Blue in the profile, but possibly black) seem to have been applied on top of pale ones, giving the impression of a narrow uneven border.

[208]: Spitfire VB EP689 UF-X, No. 601 Squadron RAF, Luqa, July 1943. Upper surface camouflage colours: Dark Earth and Middle Stone ('A' pattern); under surface colour: probably Light Mediterranean Blue.

[209]: EP689 was fitted with the much smaller Aboukir filter installation instead of the bulky Vokes fitted at the factory. Note the C above the serial number (compare p. 78) and the stencilled note 'SPECIAL ENGINE'. The Spitfire was written off in an accident on 22 September 1943, Australian F/O Alexander Blumer escaping unhurt.

210

211

[210–211, 213]: F/Lt Władysław Drecki, 'B' Flight commander in No. 152 Squadron, flew Spitfire VC MA289 UM-T several times in September 1943. On the 11th he used it when he claimed a Messerschmitt 109 destroyed during a patrol over Salerno beaches. The claim was subsequently credited by RAF authorities, but was not included in the official Polish score of the pilot, because he was killed in a take-off accident two days later and consequently failed to file a formal report for the Polish AF HQ. The photographs were taken by Harry Hoffe, a fellow pilot of No. 152 Squadron who also flew MA289 regularly (he gave them to Tomasz Drecki, F/Lt Drecki's nephew, when they met in 1996). The Spitfire was photographed at Lentini East in Sicily, No. 152 Squadron's base from July until the first week of September 1943. The aircraft is in the Desert scheme, probably with Sky under surfaces. The codes appear to be black with narrow white outline. The aircraft individual code letter must have been altered at some point, which resulted in the overpainting of the serial prefix (MA) on the port side and in the application of a rectangular background in a different colour on the starboard side.

[212]: *Spitfire VC MA289 UM-T, No. 152 Squadron RAF, Sicily, September 1943. Upper surface camouflage colours: Dark Earth and Middle Stone ('A' pattern); under surface colour: probably Sky.*

212

213